CW00548082

Contraflow

Contraflow

Fay Musselwhite

Longbarrow Press

Published in 2016 by
Longbarrow Press
76 Holme Lane
Sheffield
S6 4JW

www.longbarrowpress.com

Printed by T.J. International Ltd,
Padstow, Cornwall

Some of these poems, or versions of poems, have
appeared in the following magazines and books,
to whose editors I am grateful:
'Lode' (*Brittle Star,* Autumn 2009)
'Fire', 'Impasse', 'Path Kill',
'Losing Face', 'Boulder', 'Eggs'
(*Matter 8, 9, 10, 11, 12*, Mews Press, 2008-2012)
'At Wadsley' (*The Sheffield Anthology*, Smith|Doorstop, 2012)
'Impasse', 'Path Kill', 'Boulder'
(*The Footing*, Longbarrow Press, 2013)
'Flight from Cuthbert Bank'
(*The Companion*, Guild of St George, 2014)

ISBN 978-1-906175-30-6

First edition

Contents

for Oliver

When we're fluent
in the language of rivers and seas
let that be our currency.

Eggs

Before we come to term, are drawn
by dryness and light, we lay a store down

the way a merest swell on the pumpkin vine
holds designs to survive its own reach,

and rosebay willowherb pumps clouds.
Our finite supply of ova nestle, primed

to glide inside an opening line
as words awaiting a sentence.

Boulder

Only by bringing it home
could she get its measure.

How this was done
she doesn't remember.

She must have been drunk.
Now her favourite hunk of millstone grit

pulled from the river's bed
vested in moss and white oxalis

has swallowed the room
land-grabbed most of the carpet.

Her children inch round this cuckoo's egg,
listen to floorboards starting to give.

Contra Flow

Coaxing a skank of hair
from a slow plughole,
I'm back
ankle deep
on the Rivelin bank,
stick in hand ripped
from a mown down tree.
We're tunnelling
under a low stone bridge
through a pileup
of crashed wood re-routed
by flash floods,
freeing the bottleneck
of leaves and rocks
and bits of twig,
thrilled at the flicker
of a ripple when
a trickle licks a passage
filtering its pressure-load,
a goit to ride high
as the main drag races
down the weir.
Clear for a moment under stone –
stuck in the silted throat
and hard to swallow,
we tug, cajole
a sand-filled traffic cone
flushed down from the road.

How Rivers Begin

While a gale unravels the high ground
down in the valley birches sway
safe in their number, but for one
its moorings shallow, roots frayed –

stunted by the limestone met too soon
it tugs and writhes against that vital ratio
of height above the ground to depth below.
Neighbours keep on shouldering it home

until a ruptured ligament lurches it
out of whack, beyond their sweep –
in a landscape layered like a palimpsest
where the scars gaping high and raw

on seasoned trees shed the boughs
lazing bleary in their own last year's leaves
pre-nascent gullies on the valley floor
already host to moss and ivy spurs –

so the birch is losing grip, its bearings slide
sinews stretch to over-reach and snarl
as they let loose their load
kaleidoscoping twigs and sky

splinters screech as timbers collide:
it's hacking neighbours' limbs, slaying shoots
and saplings of its closest kin.
It comes to rest in wreckage

like an open grave.
We approach the risen face,
its root-beard clumped and dropping gritty locks,
to witness, at its nape, wood-flesh
unfurl from lacerated bark

a star of sky, and the landed birch
laying out the course
for a new earth-vein.

At Wadsley

As day bakes into the ground
we first skirt the common on the fairway side,
walk where willowherb butts sprung turf,
till we turn off to follow an old sheep wall
so moss-overgrown as to seem cloth-sewn,
through knee-high heath on paths barely seen
unless trodden on, then up by their criss-cross
to the day's full-beam, and summit-field's full pelt
takes us on into shade skittered by silvery bark,
and we lend our warmed soles to the process
of keeping the birches' uppermost roots
flush with the earth's dark surface.

When its scarring begins we descend
by the trough of a worked-out ravine,
to a trading floor of birdsong and caw,
pass ash-blown bruising where fire's been
kicked to its bones, find our way
by the tree with change beaten into its skin –
one-eighty-seven is somebody's bus fare home –
and silt only rouses to glisten and flow
in ditches' most secret creases. We lap the last
bramble patch and head through the scrub
to rise out and up on bright land
for our final leg.

*

On the top field path a young redhead starts
a wide-eyed beckoning close to a heathery edge.
Come quickly and help us she says.
You know our cousin Amy?
I don't know this girl from Eve.   I say *Yes.*
We need to call 999, she's slipped down the side.

She waves at the brow of the ridge, where gorse
and clumped grass rive in a deep yellow tongue –
a fifteen-foot fall of too friable soil, barren of all
but the wispiest twig and shallow-hooked tuft.
The solitary jut is the Amy-wrapped rock
and the grit in the twist of her joggers and top
tell the locus she drove in getting her grip.
Panic still glints in the glaze on her cheek.

To sidestep my fright at the crumbling slope
I learn the other girls' names,
then as Janice and Stephanie watch
feel out a foothold, another, I reach her,
find the right tone for the phrasing to free her,
see her unravel herself from the snag

and somehow we're all on the slide:
Amy, her cousins, my two dogs and me.
From the rearguard a glimmer
of houses and road shows the world going by
as we grapple, clutch and de-climb,
each in our own staggered time,
and we're dusting down on the flat
to find the integrity of bones
undisturbed. We straighten our clothes.

*

A week or so ago, as night's shade grew,
a couple of us shifted camera, tripod, lights
and coloured gel through waning silver birch
to abandoned ganister pits that cleave this terrain,
now claimed by local lads who ride around
their found work-and-time-made track, on bikes
fit for this: their thickset frames, and tyres
sculpted like the sun cracks land.

We glimpsed them on the woods' low edge
tearing up the dusk in a scamper-salamander
hunkering in to scale the scrub, breaking cover
at the ridge top, rag the turf, get in line to charge
down into the quarry, kick off at the knuckle,
ride the still of fluid muscle on the cooling air,
hit the ground in shadow, glide,
tug a front wheel to a broadside scuff,
pull up in a glottal stop.

Holding back, an eye out for our hollow log,
an ear to catch the rugged riders' drift,
we watched the treetops smudge and fade to black,
then we set up, and darting in and out of shot,
tricked the lens by keeping our moves quick,
stage-lit bark and moss, poured molten light
into a chamber under rocks, spilled lapis, crimson,
verdigris to shimmer up the trunks of trees,
dappled dark between the leaves,
escaped exposure every time
we captured our light-painted
outlines on the sky.

Fire

Like the outside of a cave
or massive nest containing one
incandescent egg
it gleams and crackles.

We layer on leaves and twigs
from a pile that tried to dry
through the wettest June
stacked before
a month's rain came in a single day
soaking homes in swathes.

Sodden twigs and leaves
half-parched by nearby flames
form a carapace like black lace
or a wrought iron shell
round timbers radiant again.

When its main lintel snaps
the cave cracks open
and the dome explodes.
Neon petals flit across the darkened lawn.
Ribbons of flame run for cover

over embers that remember
the robin's breast
blazing now in our dark shed
nestling her eggs
in the smoothed bowl
of layered leaves and twigs

she gathered in her beak
with moss, fallen fuchsia flower,
red and pink and once,
soft and pale as spider's web,
the skeleton of a holly leaf.

Caught

In the moments before
he touches down – on a log in the rustley brown
of overgrown grass, ruffle-shutting his fantail
like a choice hand of cards, dark beak
hooked and stone-hard, bead-eye bright,
                                    and shrugs
wings to rest round his plump speckled breast –

like flicking the switch
on an unoiled machine, the clamour begins
its hierarchy of squawked cautions:
                                    high in the birches
three magpies screech out their guttered staccato,
blackbirds report from the holly bush heart, while robins,
coal tits and finches fret in their covers.

Sparrowhawk shuffles,
somehow encumbered by his prey-bird trousers
draping too long to be the knee-breeches
commonly worn by his species,
                                    until
those low ankle-flap feathers show in a flutter

they have their own locus of organ and muscle.

Small bluster: the twig-bones of sparrow
or wren in the carriage of talon.

Goat Boy and Other Journeys

Get the skin off a mammal,
we're all much the same underneath
Susannah Gent, artist / taxidermist

Taxidermy for Beginners

As I drive, town loosens its hold, peels away
on terrain that hums the long rhythms of rain and sun
and I see how the land cleaves to its sinews,
and rolls over its own hill-bones,
how deer graze the contours that flank the M1, how a lane
trails out from a hollow where conifers tangle, down
to the palm of the farm's dappled yard.

While venison look on I park the van,
dig out the name of the abattoir man
and after some poking around, find my way in.
The shop wears health and heritage like a second skin.
I wait in stonework stillness, browse the antlers
and chalk-listed cuts. My stag heads must
be in a fridge out the back on a shelf
with steaks of themselves, or alone.

The man arrives to say *they're at the other place*
so we drive beyond leylandii.
He's high-end trade and proud, yet mild
as the voice I'd met, tells me slaughterhouse heads
are burned or released by the vet – a hasty retreat
from the scandal of putting the brains of cattle
into the other cows' mouths. Trees thin to tarmac,
I pull up at buildings, low and single storey,
they squat the shade of a crescent copse,

leak their flat light through thick polythene flaps,
blood is hose-swept to gridded troughs, hooks drop
to lap ceiling tracks with the heft of chain-held stock,
un-lidded bins over-brim in meat matter. The man
catches my eye, and in his I see I'm a slippery line –
he feeds his mind on how this everyday carnage
may flare up in mine.

He goes in one door, says he'll come out another.
Antlers lay piled like a weapons stack, blood-ended,
sawn-off and tender still in their velvet, unossified, untried.
Now he's back, pulling wide another flap to show
the trio I've come to collect.

I smooth down the van's plastic sheet,
while the man, his tongue loosened now by relief,
wants me to hear of those more vulgar than he, how it all
came to this – and I think of myself, cornered by threats
from some bar or gallery bore, and know the spur
for tales like these wasn't anything I'd done or said.
I gather up antlers and load the heavy heads.

How We Came to This

It were a trauma letting the dairy herd go.
More for me dad, I were a young man
big with me new ideas, now it's been thirty year
since our cattle and Highland deer first calved together.
Here in this meadow the gamble began and soon
the yearling fawns were putting it all on our table.

You'll get attached to an animal, mind, it can be a tangle
when you wrestle a labour of muscle, lifeline, slippery limb,
and it's coloured like a bloodshot eye.
However it is they divide you tend to remember.

So we were the breeders, and for a while the herders
from counties around trampled a track to our door,
and fat of their bankable land were all raised
by the stock pulled from our hinds.
Till the bottom fell out of that paddock.

Then some American wrote me a line,
heard of a stag I had – a sought-after creature,
called him a twelve pointer, wanted to fly
all the way over and shoot him, but I knew
by the slant of his gun on the page that he'd miss
every point of the trip, told him to offer his dollar elsewhere.

Maybe me easy-clean floor and factory lighting
make what I'm running here look like a death camp.

In the field if you want to take three or four out
put food on the ground, move back twenty yards,
they face you, their heads go down
and it's a clean shot.

When you reach around thirty or forty
it's another story: top end of the market needs
a quick bleed not animals wounded and wheeling about
in fear and mud – both are contaminants – so
we adjusted the drop-claw crush, and they
are going in for an ear-tag.

I wonder which end you'd prefer.

With me own young to feed I'd to think on me feet
I plumped for the meat.

Goat Boy

Mind your head if you're coming in.
I don't need much, so don't slip up
where my beer spilled or chips got dropped,
just a line to hang out my squirrel-skin socks,
a pot to piss in and a lamp
to turn the day off.

It's alright for her next door
swanning about in someone else's fur,
in here there's only me to stir the time about.
And always the taunt of next autumn's rut.
I'd be out like buckshot
but muscles stutter, I gulp and rust,
live on cans when they'll serve me in the shop,

don't mind if they call me things for being small
like Mothercare – except she don't no more –
long as they don't mess where my antlers used to be,
under this bandana, see, my head bears scars
of where the tender calcifies, drives violence
to its own ends and falls.

So I let them call me Goat Boy,
'cause what they don't know can't hurt me.

Oak dawn, when flesh has gone to bone
shed velvet litters sedge, drapes passing twigs
in the rise of bracken mist
above rooks' caws, blood's thunder's all I hear,
though moving nearer now, a bellow
rips the heath raw
and hind-sweet dew snags my breath.

Sometimes I climb the wall.
I'm Fawn Man, Stag Child.
Excuse me while I hang the candle out.

Now I swagger here in Bart Simpson underwear
a chip grazer in kids' threads
swigging this thin fizz in sterile streets
where a magpie may lie sleek and broken-necked
outside a dead pub's shuttered eyes.

And I'm back to when it was just he and I –
me, him and the sky and a crease of turf,
and a thirst for his girls his heft would not shift.
Out there life means life
and I'm girded still by a whiff on the haze,
the shudder-rush when weaponry locks
and the seeing-off I got.

Blood-eyed, lame, fear-blind
and on the wrong track, flank-slashed,
I fled downwind for distance and cover,
a blur of red-rimmed scrub, then spun out,
a maple-lined lane led me on
beyond the kingdom of green to run down
a brambled gutter to town.

I nibbled buddleia on wasteland rubble,
licked at a puddle,
poked out a den in this skag-end squat

to lay low, steaming, as winter kicks in
see my fine candle stuffed into rubber,
lick at the sags in my skin.

I stagger gutless, a shadow on cave walls
like her next door: no longer moored.
She rabbits on, empty inside but warm,
she don't turn from the curl in my lip,
the glass in my eye and sure, sometimes
I slip in there and drink with her, why not?

Here I spill

peat from riven rock
craw of crow or rook
I blink
shiver over stone
lick another glaze on sodden moss
pool to pool I brim
shimmer down in cataracts
I zigzag the scrub
glimmer, swell
seethe from this hill

dodge heather, tussock sedge
rinse limestone gaps
like rushing through teeth.
I taste the clough's low reach
span boulder's breadth
rewrite each dive and lash
dither, gush
writhe in tailbacks
dash along the flat.

I steam into a bend
get waylaid in a bryum glen
drawn to wallow
down moss avenues
sucked in
to a city in languor
dim lit, miniature
I sup on mulled spore soup
and lap up glamour
like a labyrinthine tureen
in thrall to gloom
I marinade

seep lower
I'm liminal
in loam eiderdown
like an opiate.
Hours mist
in least-resisting lines
I linger on fringes
gloss over local lore
go to ground
lie low in slithery ravines
lick a living tonguing grooves in lime
root out the old short cut

greet sky on knife-grey rocks
glint of future-shock
etch my name on crag's relief
I swarm sun-winked
ripple sinuous in lanes
slip into the main drag's swim
I interweave
ghost beaded shivers
peal over shallow palisades
where wagtails flit
I re-invent the drift

gulp bottlenecks of millstone grit
worry wattled roots for loam
rinse out the lode
I'm currency
I swagger wide
undercut the banks
right and left
a pulse through this heath
I'm gullible and deep.

Goat Boy staggers on

but I'm getting pulled in
to a feathery bed and a credit card
to vinegar chips in midnight bars

her-next-door wants to wash my bandana
fluff it all up in her tumble dryer
she's winding me in

I'm on the trail of gossip and rumour
mistaking a taste of white sugar
for that hind-sweet whiff on the haze

I remember the day – me, him and the sky
I can't hear the rip of the breeze for the whine
of a thousand TVs and the gnashing of tills

with their bellows and trills are telling me lies
pulling up billboards over my eyes
selling out starlight for neon signs

I can't read the news in the rustle of leaves
can't see the woods or the trees
I'm getting pulled in

to winter again in the suck of the city
now blood in my veins runs thin
I'm recalibrating to opening times

the phases of retail are turning my mind
and muscle to stuttering mush
and Special Brew nips at the back of my throat

judders its metal road deep in my gut
all there is is rubble and grit
river runs in and river runs out

I'm getting sucked in
getting pulled in.

Progress

I wake with it already on my chest.
All yesterday our homespun miasma's
unapparent flecks were bolstered, given taste
by this blow-in of Saharan dust.

Overnight the window gulped it in
pulled it through the curtain nap, now its ashen swags
cloud the room, whirl and darken in the skirting shadow
where fallen clothes bank in dunes.

Where a man in desert camo
walks out of a billow, scanning sand as though
to sow or scythe, in his eyes the plumes
of oil wells on fire.

Following behind this advancing soldier
guided by his grip on the man's shoulder
stumble-runs another figure – head bowed
as if weighed down by its lamp, cough-hunched,
blown and backlit through gusting coal-dust.

Then clinging for his life to the miner's arm
a man made of wool and mud, face sandbag-blank,
shell-strobed in rust-tinted smoke, pulls himself, his gun
and pack, from the suck of dead-man soup.

And curling his fist
round the second soldier's rifle strap, a wispy-chinned lad
flees a riverbank factory shed, pursued by the neon flash
of a gritstone blast that won't get him yet
but by stealth in the next two decades
it'll annex his vital tracks.

We wait for rain.

Trench Rat

after an episode in All Quiet on the Western Front *by E. M. Remarque*

Survivors of barbed wire,
mortar-shell crossfire, gas; for grub
we bite abandoned pets to death and harvest
soldier parts from no-man's mud.

Fed up and multiplied: now's the lull
when no-one dies, they hide
what bread they get and we are legion.

I've been slapped about, tail-spun and hurled,
for running over resting faces, trailing
what they've stashed beneath their heads.

Heard a brother on a rafter-mission
shin a roof-slung line, ride the crust
of its suspended load, tucking in –
till the slap of torch-bright
heralds rifle shot.

Tonight yeast's bitter scent is raw.

Their candles snuffed, we wait,
in our tunnelled earth
deep beyond their timber-
splintered damp of sand and sack
safe in our own smell
our old small scratchings.

Soon as they settle we inch out
guile sapped to spill over the flat,
fill our cheeks, our fists, fight,
rip the supper pile apart.

Creepers run, more come to gorge
on the soldiers' oversight
a colony in swarm, the feast
a writhing rat and bread heap…

then

FLASH

Their bayonets of light hit our backs –
we're a scrabble-whirl, a blinded scuffle-scrum
our agonies wail above rifle cracks, under hail
of metal, bread, fur and flesh scraps

when sight of the scatter-rapture
patches back: rats scurry like drain-suck
some drag a smashed leg, coats sag,
collapse on the broiling kin and crumb mush

      foot must be stuck
I pull at it: the dull limb
stays snagged

before me looms a face:
whiskers terror-sprung, eyes reaching out
then glazed

                    patterns rage
cross-beams slash, chase

        smoke-gusts blur, I slide
into emptying, lay as dead, curled
around my leaking gut, hip a gash cooling
in the stench of shot and panicked rat

which slowly sweetens as my clutch loosens
on a spear of crust, breath gutters, soft focus
smears into memory of safe belly fur
in my ear a milk-warm purr.

Adventures in Procurement

a southern city toward the end of the 1980s

Inner cities, whether they know it or not,
are crying out for more entrepreneurs
 Sir Keith Joseph
 House of Lords, May 1988

Firewood

You need good boots,
a collar to the wind, and a shoulder
braced for the brunt of a cussed load;
gloves end up half pocket-stuffed, half lost
in the woods we gather to meet each winter
night head on. Alone or in pairs by dark we go,
every day or so, for armfuls that warm us
twice at least – as we handle it home,
cleave it apart for the hearth brought to light
by peeling back years of emulsion, paper, tin
and a squatting of soot,

then we rouse in it
a thing with breath to rage against dim,
to syncopate our undertones, rid the roomscape
of straight edge and flickered repeat.
A crucible for plots incendiary and tropical,
enthralling though hard to follow:
a vapour plume flags a site of pent intensity,
battleground or stadium, factory or town,
when its cover blows, licks and lashes
make light of a community exposed,
interspersed with snapshots in deep focus
of what may lie beneath the skin or ground,
and loud reports as a barricade falls,
spits its knots to hide unchecked in rugs,
socks and feline fur.

We burn what we can find
in streets colonised by stair shifters, roof raisers,
bay window chasers, home owners performing
their open house surgery, bedrooms waiting
in polythene wings. We raid their skips
for hundred year timber whose days are up,
try our luck at the hospital new-build outcrop
for pallet or plank, and it's never enough
for the beast that gapes at our chimney breast.
While we, between chokes, stoke it to its last
bright gasp, brasher for the creep of black
pooling coolly round embers' fade to ash,
the flare shares its shine in the beeswaxed flanks
of our borrowed cello, battered piano, trove
of guitars, without it crossing a mind
to feed those darkening chambers in
to the guttering flame.

Smokeless Zone

That grass never looks enough
poking up in mud beside the paper shop,
a fenced-off corner with its billboard above,
even for a goat, yet when the man who banks

on rent for half our street (shaves his cut
from the quarters of drug traders, end users,
bird-eye way-losers, junior and mental nurses,
piss artists and degree chasers) has to service
his other god's call for a slaughter,

the small altar beast will graze
till its tether ends in this staked enclosure,
cowed in the glare of lucre's mutable prayer,
the confident fonts tightly screwed

to the casino's revolving door, while over
the inner ring road a mosque slotted itself
into the sprawl the Methodists left
at our avenue's top.

If it's late afternoon we may drift by
for licit supplies: baccy and skins,
a bag of coal, bottles of wine and milk,
beans at the store with a tribal name
(keeping their foot on the pulse).

This is our smudge on the map, our folds
of the city's inskirts, a skip to the new
asylum, a hop from the drop-in and dry-
out house, and at our road's bottom: bare-

legged kerb-girls cluck in the gutters,
and world-famous *please ring* models wait
in lit windows to make ends meet, some days
their sailors queue up that street.

Our payload must've gone down in
the boats we gleefully burned, so what
floats us is an ear to the sound:
time is the lag between beat and the next,
chords progress, high notes sustain

us giro to giro, low notes stretch
and tangle with our blithe refrain
stoked by a smoke ever harder to get,
and you know: I don't pick or blow,

I knit to fill in the gaps, now this
break in the market has my name on it,
a chain of demand with scales of its own
a new shade of yarn to my bow.

Wearing the Trousers

When reluctant warriors roll their trashed homes
onto our street to lick their welted wounds we shudder
at the babble of a beanfield battle; when change

buckets rattle we chuck cash for scrapped families
at pit towns far off; while our donkey jackets
are ironic, down by the railway track

a billboard shoved up by the DHSS shows the beating
of round pegs square, as I step into my new career –
though before I still my needles,

cover the Singer, or shut the material drawer,
out of a length of don't-mess-with-me cloth
I cut accordingly and stitch myself up

trousers for the job with deep hip pockets, each
to hold a nine-bar snug. I slip a riff or two from home
behind my ear, and go to work

down a market run on half-caught rhyme and swagger,
never clear on passage, time, notes or measure
even whether: bother stay or come back later.

Keep my nerve and humour powder-dry,
heed only the flame-yield aroma,
and how it teases out in thumb and finger.

Tuned to an undertone, the city shifts its grid,
racks focus on a rampant pulse of merchandise
channelled through a chain of tea-oiled gaffs

tucked away above a sullen café, in the lee
of a storefront harbour for shy antiques,
or the weigh and sack room of a wholefood shop.

When a black Moroccan deal sours in a rumour
of henna steeped in alcohol, or homegrown mashed
in shellac and cooking oil, I need tiding over –

I beg a ride out of town on an iffy whisper,
get the run around a low-rise warren, lose my lift
to a snakebite sofa and a spliff of snide,

pass a man unloading spirit in his drive,
bus it back, draw a blank at the market flats,
in despair try the angels – no joy there,

sound the neighbours out, then the laid-up trailers,
follow a beat from a bar to the narrow house
with paint-splashed stairs – those splatters

leap like embroidered flowers, the landing
reels in a potency that relishes day's end in reach,
and the burn I bring home is sweet.

Tales from Min's and Other Storeys

Cornered in concrete, a breeze whips the block,
competes with two hi-vizzed sweepers for the scattering:
a TV in smithereens.

One leans on his broom, tuts
at the other: younger, moon-walking his awe at fallen stars.
The older keeps a skyward eye as gusting plastic,
mangled metal, cells of shattered screen rush
at the man handing me the door,

I spiral up the concrete stairwell,
and my footsteps reverb – I can hear them
gaining on me half a floor below.
At the landing I push on through the wired glass
to carpet that clings to my soles,
a grin for Min's spy-hole and I'm in.

Inside it's window-watching, tea and chatter,
faces gather, those who missed the TV
saw the video that followed, I squeeze
in next to Donna, listen

as Stephen, reminiscing, mimics his dad's fury
that slung: first the curling tongs then two dozen
Motown singles he shared with his sister
one by one into the river,

and Nuala murmurs, raw as yesterday,
how her brother once despatched to the canal
her Abba-smitten Dansette Player,

while laid slack behind his propped designer flip-flops,
Mikey, in his up-all-night-indulge-me rattle,
begs the tale of Min's recent evening with her kin.

She tells of how dining was all but done,
and banter beginning to slur, when they snagged
on the local whoring habit –
                                          muttered huffs had tried
to let it slide, but Min weighed in, siding with the harlots' lot
till a chill rose up to thin and hush her flow,
then through the arc of her sisters' loaded glances,
heard her mother snort – *Well, we all know about you.*

Stunned for a beat as the cadence sunk in,
Min caught on, leaped up quick and hot – *Shame is
that I never said – it's weed I trade not flesh.*

Like tearing down drapes, she saw how dark
it had been, in the furrows fleeing her mother's face,
how deep a silence can go, and her widening gaze
met eyes anew through the liquor in glasses,
and from under lashes not raised to her in years.

A month on and Min still holds that day's glow,
from the mirth in her cheek's tilt to the candid turn
of her toes, gracious in her wonder at
her family's pros and cons, she chuckles,
and keen as ever to everyone's needs – *Terry,
will you fill the kettle?*

And on it goes.

Last weekend dawn raiders came in vain again
in their size tens, distressing all her settled things,
shrugged as if to smirk off into the morning sun,
but Min's tongue had not forgot their copper's knock
and went at them till they coughed up a docket
to ward off their gratuitous return,

this she keeps in mind beside the tally
of her two piles: one is her rinsed savings,
in the other, timbers rot to let Kilkenny rain pool
on flagstone floors, creeping up supporting walls,
hailed by buddleia in masonry left to her
when the tumour outgrew her man,
and she packed his paintings, sold his books
and bottles, swaddled his daughter
to follow her migrated clan.

Within this stack of stories, that girl's grown,
and now her own girl is Min's mornings:
their songs and drawings, her games
of teddies, tins and old pennies,
before business begins, her shelf
low in the alcove she calls *granny's shop*,

where Min now beckons me and plays
her kitchen scales for my four ounce block.

Leon

      levels two log seats
at the fire's leeside, props his can,
rests a saucepan to simmer over embers,
and in reaching for the spatula he fashioned
in his first sky-ceilinged week, reignites the burn
of some unguarded workday turn or snag –
by savouring its ache he recognises each tenderness
of muscle, breach of flesh as a grace note,
a repose-echo of toil that melds him to the land.

No shame or shy away: these wounds no more
the tracks and blooms left by pokes,
her tiny stone-clawed fists, or falling into things;
nor from when a long-surrendered flame
sent her man and brothers round to get him out,
they van-bundled and cottage-bound him till
his humours ran clear, and only then
let him take the chainsaw in hand.

*

At the edge of sound always the road
where a rumble peels off and swells
through the dusk-sprung hums and creaks
of forest settlement. In a lull the fire
sighs and spits, Leon picks grass flecks
out the thickening broth, hears his supper guest
drop a gear to lean into the scrub,
ride to a crescendo and pull up – cooling ticks
fall in like a soloist's ebbing tones
with the waking whispers
of the woods' nocturnal risers.

Don't you miss a bit of it? The bands,
the bars, those city lights…

                            Ha –

smoke eddies as the curve of Allegra's spine
strobes again behind Leon's eyes, his name
on her colonial tongue in his mind's ear.

When I kicked the brown on my last long stretch
I was never going back.

Leon tells the lumberjack how deep and snug
the bench he rigged up in the off-licence flat,
of the first guitar he fixed for cash,
the mixing desk he grew from bartered labour,
rescued parts, the nip of solder to tune a sharp heart,
tricks for greasing old machine heads,
cork saxophone pads, and mixing live jazz, that a bass
more sublime than any he knew drove the pulse
for an all-girl art-school punk band, in the hands

*

of Allegra, who'd fled the ladies' college
favouring a rougher finish, kept her distance
from Tobago where her father bristled,
pulled out charcoal, drew herself
into Leon's chiaroscuro.
And after her pickups were realigned,
the wah-wah back in her step, Allegra stayed.

But the neighbourhood's musical wounds
yielded a living too meagre for two.

So, what am I supposed to do
when a nine-bar kisses the bench
with mention of a stack in tow? And you know
how those musos blow.

He dovetailed his enterprise: found time
for body and mind to entwine.

She played and drew
while I kept the plates going round.

Till one afternoon two came balaclavaed,
gun-pointed Leon flat to the floor, he'd been slack
as one pulled the rug on a board neatly cleaved,
bagged up hashish and cash; they went too far
when the other began packing punters' guitars.
Leon had none of it: gun to his leg, he said *leave it out,*
you got what you came for now fuck off.

Next he heard: their rubber burned to the road.

Getting home from drawing life, Allegra's head
spun and clarified: her sabbatical at an end, she replied
to the childcare needs of her mother's New York friend.

*

Without her Leon sunk like a stoner,
diminished to the bole of his being, on course
for his own felling, but held by an augmented seventh
looping around a demented bass rhythm, he rallied,
met a trade wind with the grim wit to haul himself up,
scrape his stake back; odds on he'd've slipped
into his groove, then Paula crawled onto the street:
four foot eleven in shades of denim, a cliff edge
of rock on each finger.

Trailing good weed, she stumbled on Leon and knew
she'd hit on her mission-vessel: she brought him
a trumpet duffed up beyond saving; begged he try,
while she raked his sorrows, rekindled old cravings,
slithered into his fenceless places, drowned out
his sustaining acoustic with tales of her platinum years –
how life on the gold-line had led to high-flying
with gems on the inside, the swank of a cigarette lit
from a ten pound note, her calf-length zebra-skin coat
she'd still fit having garnered no weight.

She poked around, derided his home, now plundered
of all residue but her patina, and soon moved him
into the rooms underneath her.

*

How easy I fell for that ramshackle plot
at the end of the terrace, how willing I was to be led
up her fetid front garden,
in through the shot-pitted door
to the hallway that swallowed me whole.

Don't miss the dark that poured down those stairs
from her wretched ruin, the thud of her slippers
a foot from my ceiling.

Leon unravelled in that galley of shadows,
lost to blown bridges and warped headstock thread,
and under his meddling landlady dripping
her solutions into his ear, began the slide back
to the old tom-foilery, till he turned
from the workbench, let her weigh his tools in.

*

Paula got Leon a runaround motor, and sent him
to mine little earners from clearance-sale rubble:
showed him prices for Burleigh Ware, Lalique
and Clarice Cliff, said he had flair, but his eager eye
alive to sound's flow, to the action of steel on fret
to within a hair's breadth remained untrained.

He'd scour the city and half the county for gear
– that one-stop drop in a brown paper wrap –
rather than digging through ancient shed skin
and auction despair for a fix he couldn't divine.

While always at home a tinkling rattle
of snide ceramic mocked his every footfall.

*I don't miss the niggling snare of those relics
or muffled reports of her overhead dramas –*

bruising the furniture, cursing the names
of glass-fronted faces that follow her – children
who learned to call somewhere else home.

*I don't miss her croak in my ear,
the tick of her laugh, her creak in the chair.*

*Don't miss how her lips
would twist a grin down when paying again for the gear,
or the flick of her hair as I bit the belt for a vein while she
smoothed a foil square, and I dug myself
darker and deeper, too deep into her.*

*

Leon reaches for the spatula, his shoulder
recalls the day's labour, and he remembers
the brute tenderness of those near-strangers
who pulled him, battered and septic, jewel-fist mottled,
from that splintered wreckage: the crockery,
the smashed-up mixing desk they found him at.

He stirs the broth, realigns smouldering logs
under the blackened pot to keep it on an even keel,

serves up.

Lesser Common Rustic

At my elbow I hear a faint judder
of something soft, spring-loaded, in trouble
in the windowsill clutter. I shift an old bottle,
lift a plant pot to uncover an earth-coloured moth
seized in the struggle to shake off a rough
fur cape of dust and disintegrating web,
though his panic-flapping only whips it up
to wind it closer in.

I make an open grab, moth quivers, still
hemmed in, his wing-breath winnowing my palm
as I pull clingy clumps from a blur of parts.
Wary of a snag or pixel smudge, I pick
at house-lint steeped in tar left by the spider's snare,
which, it seems, grew stickier as structure failed,
till the tiny living dynamo can shed his last
shreds of robe. I barely see him go.

Moorhen

Of the bird you pocketed last summer
to drive one-handed home, I remember
little but how sheer the tender sheen
on long probing toes and legs, slippery to grip,
delicate and wilful as a clutch of baby snakes.

A versatile design of pale lime scales
had been messed up, intercut with twine, a threat
to paint-thin skin tightening on flesh
bloating out between the hobble-net, like whey
through a straining cloth, or an overspill
of thigh above a stocking top.

Darkening her face, you held the creature still.
I fetched my strongest glasses, lacework scissors,
nuzzled steel under the bind, each snip a risk
– the dainty blades like tailor's shears
snapping round our whippet's leg –
unravelling the lazy fisher's web.

Half my task was palming off her squirmy stride,
as filaments of limp nylon piled,
flesh refilled itself, and her limbs flexed
their prehistoric elegance, lithe again and free
of any scathe to skin or feather
when you slipped her back into the river.

Mint

I can't name the kind, filched from scrub that keeps
allotments from the riverside, sprigging up
among the dock and clover, heads of seeding grass
and cornflower. I spied it from the path, a measured tug
taught the rain-soaked ground to yield me four rooted spines.

While they find their feet in steeped kitchen leavings
mashed with earth-mud, they miss the shoulder to shoulder
race for light, the river's snigger, listen for the thwack
of dog-sticks on the bank.

Leaves that arrived pale and downy, darken
and glaze; edges crisp. There are casualties:
one then another stem stiffens and frays; one wavers
before firming up to its new terrain. The other flexes in the sun,
and at each nook where jaded leaves hang limp, a tongue
of pale green fur pushes out and bifurcates for the next
tiny shimmer-spur to poke through.

No longer can I ditch the pocked
and ugly hangers-on, render pupas homeless, let birds
and spiders go unfed – this pot
is like a tenement block site: some leaves locked tight
with secret nurseries inside, some curl like shawls

or sleeping bags round those who lay about
in corridors to sleep or change, away from dust-blown webs
strung out plant to fence, a spider punctuating each.
A stealthier arachnid without net patrols the heights
on sprung-thread legs, thin enough to masquerade as cracks
in paint or wood; its body, like a pumice bean,
nestles where they meet.

Yesterday a caterpillar, green and fat, breakfasted on mint,
this afternoon I saw it spiralled beneath. Either it's moved on,
been lunch or swallowed in the dusk; unlike these two flies,
the size of sunflower seeds, orange, neon-bright,
copulating on a leaf.
                                    As they pump they walk, or rather
she walks halfway round the serrated edge, he rides her
as she fly-hops leaf to leaf; if they were people
they'd've gone at it back door to attic rafters,

where they rest,
                            at the poke of an iris spike, still engaged.
A closer look shows both
diminishing: as between their potent ends – her gape,
his taper – underneath him, joining them, a sac balloons.

Their pulse abates, her wings flick, hands fidget at her face; he drops
his head, his wings lay side by side, flat.
                                    Do they sleep?
Enjoined nearly an hour, now. A linger,

then she's up, gesturing, shuffling her feet; again they pump
to fill their sac, then he bulks up, takes his own weight
yet remains attached, and for a moment holds
a foot of hers in each of his (do they kiss?) then finds his way
behind. They're end to end like dogs, stomping
on the tall leaf tip, till she slips round the back to grip
the underside; through leaf their feet touch.
                                    Soon

urgency subsides,
                   and they divide. A bead of glisten crowns
his point, another seals the sac which seems to ruffle into her;

she waddles about. He wanders downward, slow
as from a taxing day, she looks his way, does she
watch him go?
                As he sidesteps onto mint, she sets off
to follow down the narrow leaf, he paces, trudges back,
is at the leaf-edge to see her pass, we both watch
her recede, dark into the iris heart.

Pulling Balsam

We veer off the verge, duck under its palisade boughs,
rope-walk the drop from the road into woodland
disturbed.
                    On the back rise
of a millpond's forgotten estate a settlement grew:
pillared in sycamore, blackthorn and birch, turning the soil
for neighbouring nettle and bracken to annex untrodden ground,
round the sagged terraces. As snake-headed bramble
laced through the thickening, mosses furred root-knuckles,
fallen limbs and exposed stone – the contours
of maps drawn in the minds of beetles, spiders, voles.

Till an insurgency blew in, snagged in the lick
of the river below to bed down, and in a year
a stand of spring-loaded blooms delivered guffaws
of particulate clusters to land-grab more bank each summer.
They shoulder over bracken and nettle, cowbane, moon carrot;
prehensile roots, like claret talons in any loose scuff or leaf matter,
grip and grow. By now a season's leap from the road.

Tonight we go at it, wise to the tide
of ripening fruit, we uproot and deflower; lay out limp hanks
of stalk-flesh to wither in trees. We tread the collateral damage:
bramble, cowbane and nettle, littered on the crosshatch
of paths hacked or sickled for access.

In a courtyard clearance effected last weekend, a seeping
of cleavers web-weaves its claim like netting a family slain.

Breaking only to bundle each hundred-stem armful, we hack
and pull, hack and pull into twilight,
make for our rope in the last light to exit
the massacre village.

In the Absence of Salt

She wonders about getting away,
flattens herself slimmer than a pay packet
to hide in the slats of a heron's wing.

Cruising a fir-lined brook upstream
she concertinas in as he weaves
the spine-curve to meet treetop slots.

Low in a knuckle-white sky, the sun
light-feathers the current's skim.
Heron cuts through, they cleave the pale gloom

suspended in dew and spore, a clammy wrap
conjured by sunrise from the night's brew.
When grip's lost to slime she drops

pitches up on glistening ribbed rock,
shivers for breath supine on the gritstone slab:
lichen-iced, cold as shoulders, veined

like marble in slathered bracken root
which she reads like runes, asking it why
in dreams, does she keep leaving beaches

drawn inland by riparian birds,
and why all her words still lie
sucked under sand by a year's hissing tide.

Memoir of a Working River

1

Old man, liver-brown
spittle-flecked and slower now retired
quits a time-worn groove, waives his bed
returns on a crow's route to Rivelin Brook.

In the coupled hut, his back
to Oaking Clough, lights a found candle stub
packs a pipe, sucks tepid dregs from a flask
beholds inner dark where he'll spill his last
and as dusk nestles lies foetal on stone.

A low wind moans in the heather
wheezes its way round the moor
whistles a twist in the ridge path's mane
grinds its name into bridge metal.

Old man shivers in skin leaf-thin
between gritstone and age-tender bones.
Remembers a sleeping bag, grimy slack
glimpsed in the last candle light
and shunned, lest dim sight miss
in its ripples some needle or blade.

Cold sludges his veins: now maybe
he'll risk that sly body sack
so flexes stiff knuckles, finds it
slimy-damp yet surprisingly thick.
Drawing it to him liberates spores
of its secrets, fungal and faecal, he bundles
the wad under shoulder and hip
and facing the night as silvery pillar
counts weirs and culverts till sleep.

Tomorrow he'll fill the river-pen
then, on the hut's inner skin
between *Darren loves Shaun*
and *Pakis go home* he'll begin.

2

He dreams Water Board Man pedalling
out to the dam in the slant of weather
to chain his boneshaker, pull on
creaking wet-wear, overground it
to the reservoir shaped like a star.
Lean in to measure its level, do battle
with sluice gate drag, then be rewarded:
while his galoshes and sou'wester pool
on the hut's flagstone floor, on the hob
a kettle steam-sputters.

In sleep's deeper reaches he gushes
through hill's inner byways to deluge
lost aquifers drained and arid for years
quenches their fissures, laps ceilings
seeps into pervious crags, listens and follows

the husk of a murmur to chambers below
where limestone spirits take form as a chorus
of cutler-mill workers in moss-leather jerkins
astride at the grind, joins their stridulous tones
spits sorrow alongside those broken men
some who sing with their face half gone
or raise a lone arm to the wheel, adds his own
to their song of exploded stone.

3

When he wakes in the dank of dawn's
south-westerly shade stiff and alone
snagged in the echo of their refrain
are snatches of his juvenilia –

...rain or spring water needs but a crease
a stem or lost limb, porous and prone, a scuff
to convene and set off. In time
a rivulet licks out a gulley and probes
ever lower so unriven ground yields a valley...

He rises

as fluid, refleshed in nascent form
slithers a slip over threshold's lip

splashes his face among tussock sedge
glazing a vein in the sponge of spent leaf
leaving a slick, angles headlong in peat

elbows through heather, reaps the scrub-dew
checks rotten boughs for rain hoarded beneath
etching a groove a niche in land's crust
cleaves a ravine to the crag's lower reach.

Spurred to rive, driven by drive, lives by renewal
raises tree roots from dark soil manoeuvres
releases loose boulders, un-snuggles stones
making their earth bed his own.

Bolder with each rill and runnel he meets
rinses sheer drops, begins to sculpt rock
jostles the silt that cradles hill-bones.

Where mosses cluster he lingers
plunges his fringes between them, plumping
their sprung vegetation before pushing on.

Feels shadow-shivers of yet-to-meet bridges
as banks either side rise to guide him he shudders
shy-slithers at whispers from plains of kept water
slips by under tall sandy pines

to greet sky again as ribbon through pasture
a slaking for flitters and grazers, a cool magnet-shimmer
for heron and otter an opportune platter

where bracken hangs over as predator cover
a nursery pool for frog larvae.

4

Now within hearing a granular mumble
persistent throat-clearing
the shifting of plates to a radical gear:
hears in the turning of corn into flour
a clarion call to the grind.

Eager in muscle he ripple-limbers
gulps up distance, ducks to tunnel the road

flushes his load into some managed arena.
Brick channelled, dammed by stone, surges on
towards spume-crested brink of unknown
where chaff sloughs off to white-tumble a weir

while the risen elite, fleet
silver-lick shifting, race-keen
is chicaned to a side lane

to slip along thinly, spit gravel, he's shallow
arrives in a vast mud-lined vessel – pent
seething, he swells.

Held molecules eddy, spin restless, and more
spill in, as to a hiring fair.

He who only knows *go* treads water
the light he fledged to follow falters
skim drifts upwards.

Men at his edges hover and probe
their cloth limbs lurch without fluency
yet they have him caught.

Gravity ushers life-salt down, he bloats
slack-lapping stone, billows as silt spirals below
bleeds in till he brims

begins to sense an old urge in the loin:
direction and drag reborn, shiver-ripples, is drawn
blurts his sleek head before tail's warned, issues
rides a high flume fresh and free, then the slap –

planks of dead tree in the face, he's hobbled
sloshed into slots, he must shoulder-shunt paddles
the roar of more of himself pushes on
snorts, gob-splutters, sees capture's cause

reflects it all as he falls:
better to be the wheel's master
than its yoked surf.

5

Springing from harness, fear and fury
grip as skin, braid and bind this skein of him
in human form to land flesh-heavy on cobbled stones
into the valley he footprints the bank.

Learns lung and bone, the motion of limbs
tunes ear and eye-lines in and slows
lets his mind load.

High on a hillside beasts graze
he knows their heat and weight, the taste
of field on their tongues and clod-straggled coats
yet how the land was carved half-forgets.

As he runs on between river and mills
fathoms the rhythm of dam – wheel – building
the hydraulic logic of currency storing
sees river abstracted by weir-head plunder
the portion lured into the goit soon halted:
a stockpile of muscle surrounded.

And the trick he most sorely remembers:
when men lift a sluice gate the river emerges –
he looks away as it gushes triumphant

– bash-splatter served up as fast fodder
into the gullets of that wooden wheel.

Kneels by a tail-race to witness
the homeward run of washed-out water.
Fingers linger, tender to the tired flow
tries to recall how this wasn't always its way.

Resolves to untangle his belly's grumble
succumbs to slumber

dreams rivers of lambs delivered
by goit to lakes of dam-nation.

6

Woken by some beast's nudge then stunned
at the incredible stillness of sky, slips in
to bathe where the mill-dam overflow cascades
slithers out freshened, rises and shivers
watches the mud where new droplets nuzzle.

Donkeys trudge by, pressing on, faces low
as if the cinder track hears their moan.
Follows their swagger-loads
sees motion onward driven
by the momentum of raw and wrought iron.

Wavers as they near the spark-shed
shy of its screaming grind and gritty guffaws
but the torture rack, humped on its back
in full watery swing, pricks his learning's gap.
Keen to find why the wheel must turn
braves the factory door

steps in and into a gusting blur
tastes its metal, feels particulates snag in sweat
takes a moment to see where he is.

In geometry against nature's grace
humans are caught in a web
each slumped over oak, held by spindle and belt
to a stone that spits hot grit.

His feet itch.

He swerves a man dragging iron rods
and trying to make his free hand speak.

On the river-run some images stick:
flashes of crimson through blackened fur shreds
on that donkey's neck, the clench of combat
riddled through men's backs.

Lying on a weir
to rinse metal squeals from his hair
on the air a tang
enthrals the inner juices –

he paces it downstream, tracks the prey
to a tufted cove, a pail propped in rocks
a man doubled over racked in rasp-spasms.

When coughing releases its grip
he sits near the man, asks how life is.

Sunk in the chest, not quite
sitting up, the man shares his snap
and between pneumatic seizure
tells how he offers blunt steel to grit
till it's flayed by resistance to its leanest edge
how each day he enters the valley
more of it enters him.

The man says he's seen eighteen summers
a grinder for three, and nails in a voice hollow-loud
what binds the wheel's turn to that cheese and bread.

Twice the man says – *Tha mus'ave a name.*
Only once – *Come wi' me, if tha needs a crust.*

7

At the snarl's core
led to an idle grindstone
in dumb show he's shown
how to catch the grit's turn
and yield to the scythe blade's curve.

In the spangled flecks thrown up
where matters meet, sees sun-needles
burn through sky-leaves, gathered glints
of star and storm unfurl, in orange blush
iron's darts lick his old trough.

Deep in the wailing screech, his life
in distorted playback: roar of loose rock, moss's seep
a wind whips the bank to surf his ripple-neck
nesters peep, rapid drops crash, creatures scream
in the grip of sex or death. Less often
a felled tree cracks – then it all stops

– a flaw or rare seed, a grenade
millions of years snug in gritstone
roused by this day's judder splits its host
lashes out in missiles of sheered rock.

A human shriek rising
in the sudden hush means
the grinder lives, though seldom whole
in eye and limb nor in full blood.

Whether that or the grateful prayer
of a long last rattle

tomorrow they'll lower in fresh stone
astride it by evening, brother child or wife
will stoop to its sneer.

8

At first he lays his head
where bryum furs a shale ledge
tucked in a bank of the old bedside
but when they turn the wheel all night
and river whispers too low to soothe
rents a bunk at the cowman's shack
lulled by the gossip of trees.

Each workday the same raw insistence
carries in its sub-cadences
the echo of a long lost argument.

Wiry and fleet, urgent, lean –
in dreams weighs scythe's sweep
through hay and sun's light drift
but knows his home is where hills meet.

Between grinding shifts he climbs
up beyond farms to quarries, brickyards
and houses strung out in rows, some alone
swathed in iron or wilderness tamed, then one

with an open door to a parlour laid out
in nature's shed gifts: feathers, bones
the bark a of tree, and likenesses
of characters, mountains, seas. He palms
a slither of limestone, traces the veins
blossoming its surface, rests it back
to its still life on inlaid table.

Back in the valley he pockets the foreman's pencil
salvages scrap from the paper-mill track
then settles in a hillside dry-stone hollow
to capture the smoulder at land's furrowed crease.

Hand learns to say what eye sees, lines flow
from timid to loaded, tributaries convene
overlay, oxbow, ripple out to show a river's flanks
grazed and reaped, to crosshatch the grief
of a ravine cleaved by time's cow-licks,
in growth's name imposed on, enclosed
then stripped.

Some risen fleck of iron or grit jags his throat
as chest heaves he tunes to those inner channels
locked open by scalded erosion, hears their pleas
and before the coughing takes hold, dissolves.

9

Fluent again
glazes wall stone
sluices its crevices, floods
an apron of field, puddles mud
and wallows

gravity draws him on into darkening loam
where tussock roots tangle with mushroom toes
he fattens seeds, rinses soil and stone, soaks
lower, snuggles deeper, inches slower

reaches a rocky layer moving freer
elbows a way through sand and rubble
sinks a gulley in clay plateau slurry lunges on
heading for light where he spills –

parting the grass that stands up to him
the rest he draggles flat, bears a smattering
of gravel and leaf matter, plunges the bank
splash-lands back to his own currency.

No more a straggler he interweaves
merges surge with an incoming brook
writhes in the sunshine, dives with ducks
rough-tumbles, huddles round rock
probes his own murk's depth, limbers up
chases dragonflies, renews his right to rive.

Getting in stride his mind unravels
thoughts slip moorings some catch hold
in weir-head cobble, shale or stone
notions nestle, nouns go to ground

puzzles of human lore resolve
or snigger away as filigree foam –
leaked from grinders' homes
he tastes their broth beer and sweat
forgets the pact they make.

All he retains is the verve
of riding those lines
releasing mind onto page.

10

After gritstone the wooden wheel's turn
is a tenable grind, he cedes to its bloat
prides in full throttle overdrive
gets the tailrace home in time to freshen up
touch fluid with kin, commune, run as a tide
before drawn on to drive again.

But tithes soon grow
beyond the logic of nature's *no* –
he wanes, men measure and curse, do deals
to stagger his progress through twenty wheels
kettle him in till he begs to work.

Mill to mill he limp-trickles, listless, resigned
always behind, a cough he can't shake is tickled
by metal, and bile seeded by grind's caustic salts,
caught in the skirts, flushed like a dose
shimmers unearthly tones, in stretches
barely veins the crease.

Men furrow their brows
murmur of cholera in the town,
and up at his juvenile shallows he drains
through lakes to slake their multiplied thirst.

Not up to the game, no mind
to escape, yet these days in power
are numbered: wheels start to stall
mills one by one fall dark silent still
goits silt, sluices rust, humans go.
Shed-wood sags then land-slapped loads
lay open broken cold, stones roll.

Nature seeps her slither-claim
of roots and rot, rinses dross.

He recoils buckles and retches
goes sick, creeps along ditches
still gets called in, draws on
hard-won resources.

More than ever he relishes rain
dances to match its lashes, embraces tirades
sucks snow and drizzle, guzzles on gulleys
slugs every drop in the valley.

Semi-retired, dilutes detoxes
cultivates gardens in goits and tunnels
rakes over scarring for relic and seed
liberates rubble, flushes out shame
to the city downstream.

Mills towards his extremity
serve retreating trade so woodland creep
spur of scree or silt gets curtailed.

Now and then a damful is levied
to pool, ride a wheel, race home
and passage is paid.

11

Trees steal back to comfort healing land –
banished for centuries by grind's fear of flame
– as wheel-gates close he's dappled again.

Birch and willow roots hug banks
probe his brick-clad flanks for pliant earth
straddle riven weirs where leaf-rafts mass
and blown grasses wattle island-clumps –

curbed by old demands he tacks and clogs
till near-choking on bracken and sapling
men and women bring dredgers, and pledges
to rescue canopied flow.

Valley hazed in his patina –
walls of mottled russet, culvert, cobble
slathered wheel-gape, spindle, stray grindstone
laze, decay, forgiven by lichen and moss.

Leisure won, reaping rivulet and brook
gush-gurgles a seasoned meander, serene
in mill-bone swagger, groove ever deeper
each trickled fissure each bevel familiar

living reminder of holloway treader
safe in his channel, one muscle
rippled to dwindle-tip – that hair-root lick

high in moorland peat cleaved a rift
steep enough to raise a dream of steel
bore labour pains, survived the crusade
that grew a settlement its global stake.

12

Humans from the city rivers made
pace his paths, leave messages
in plastic wrappers bottles cans
he chatters news as they pass

washes dogs, offers ball or stick swaps
ducks to chase on dams filled as lakes
fish to borrow and weigh, currents to test
children's minds and limbs –

for budding explorers a course
engineers a ductile force
poets a thousand metaphors.

On he pours, wrinkled skin-glisten
shore-level disguise for still heron
catches the tint of kingfisher's glimmer
the fan-flare as air kisses iron.

And below where dippers grip his ribs
wade in, hunt bedrock bugs
inner currents keep his longest job
pursue the vital mission to unveil
caress, render to the atmosphere
each layer of his muse.

Sprightly yet wide old man, liver-brown
spittle-flecked lens at land's crease
through trees reflects all he's known –
limestone forest grit.

13

Suburban now, a glimpse between roads
telling the flow of journey's lode
tongue with tale's germ on its tip.

Niggled by another's deeper pulse closing in
senses this uncoiling roar will take his all

a purge – as any brook rill or burn
he ever met spilled their histories to him –
at this watersmeet the mouth is his.

Last shake of his froth-head –
recalls a downhill freefall
a wheel, how he leapt
memory rides in on reason's tide

surge rises, bores the last bend
bails out at the last weir's crest
on grass he shimmers into human skin

watches the Loxley usher his kin
through palisades, into the throng

and on, under the bridge he scales.

Flood Triptych: The Loxley

1. Long Fallow

Across the lake, a car's slotted radiator plate lounges in oak
on a stump in clumped spikes of growth.
Scraps of broken sled jag the river's steep flank,
light slips through sky-leaves to silver-bead the weir
and on to channel fern, oxalis, sycamore and dandelion
swathing out in colonies seeded in earth-memory
of shedded souls offering metal to the wheel. Trees here
seem weak: trunks rot, crease-drop their column-loads
at land's meet, or ten feet up; the breach a ragged tuft.
In the under-dank, grey slabs nestle weather-hunched,
pitted, stacked, and harnessed still by iron bolts,
left to slow, stoic hosts to moss-creep. Roots plait,
and probe the un-worked ground. Skirting pools
of bright brown mud, they interlace the bank, are undercut,
or rise above the flow – low enough to snag on leaves,
bits of twig and, as if a flood's been through, clothes
like and not like those washed out from grinders' homes.
Knotted in the wattle-growth: a scarf, a shoe, a sock,
trousers, baseball cap; a black umbrella, noble, stalled,
its gown slashed to petals, ribs rusted slack,
tall among sprung shoots, a toehold in stone.

2. *Factory*

When you scrabble over mangled girder,
ruptured brickwork, giant bones of timber
– to clamber into somewhere money's made its own
hunkered in, tamed the ground, occupied the sky,
traded its mutations then moved on,
leaving what remains to blister through its rubble phase –
birds announce your trespass with egg-nest urgency,
a pigeon bolts the cover of a sagging slated rafter,
squawks as into a patrol transmitter.

        The party's clearly over:
underfoot the silted scuffle of industry unravelled.
Kick a nozzle-can, it scuttles like the husk of a vivid fruit –
its lettering's the late florescence of this settlement.
In ragged sunlight buddleia casts shadows on mosaics
of landed masonry – softer than the angles etched
by unleashed metal, dead and fraying leaded cable –
grasses knit their root-mats in crevices,
a bee-queen prospects for an opening.

3. Little Matlock

When the valley convulses like a full-term muscle
and you wake to weather oncoming, unfathomed,
its thundering snarl in the rooms underneath,
as it ransacks your chattels to bolster its terrible bulk,
it glugs in the chimney, raid-rattles the dresser.
Still it comes, quaking the sleep from your man,
slamming its tyranny up through the ceiling

to lap at your feet till pools lake, bedclothes float,
and mud is your slither-rug. Icy and damp
at your nightgowned hip the chamber wall is in spasm,
and braced against the room's rumble, your husband
shield-cradles the boy-bundle, yet you can't know

that this ram-rabble is waters broke free
and the crackle you hear of the hillside on fire
is really the wrenching of trees, like hair
snatched by the handful, where river banks buckle
and dread-water towers to tear up the land.

Nor can you know how when you wade waist-high
your home will turn in a twist of its timber-torso,
pluck from its quivering roof-nest a beam
to stagger your man, back-beat and uncurl him
for the surging swell to unburden him. The drag
in his fist of unravelled blanket, as your child
shedding his last lamb-sheet, leaves on the tide.

The Ache

This grit-boned city
crucible for light conspiracy
forged in the collusion
of architecture with terrain
sustains the craving
for an edge more elemental
lapped by the world's currents
yet more singular than this
craggy inland tendency
for each drop
to rise again.
Rumours mill
in cavities half-seen
beyond the church or cinema
the ring road's brow
of a gape
or breathing space, a release
from urban circuitry
a surge in focal reach
a falling away so final
it has to be the sea
licking the backs
of that wall of shops.

Drift

From a bench of buffed granite – its surface flecked
with ash and gunmetal grey, warmed by midday –
I watch the wrong door of a boat-fronted building
in fine brushed stone and glass the colour of peat-laden river,
in my pocket the disc you said you'll translate.
A gust blows up off the station as though from a beach.

If it were sand and sea down there, the blast
to my shoulder and cheek would be salt-fresh, while this
is hand-dryer hot: those fountains announcing
the railway approach have no reach, and this valley's flow
is the GO STOP SLOW of so many lanes on tarmac and rail.
Homes pile up the other hill.

You track me by phone, step out from an edge in the glass
to walk alongside a reflection of billowing cloud.
I fish out the disc and offer it up, you grin
at my failure to take direction in where to wait,
finish your cigarette and slot back into the prow of the block.
In your hand: pictures of rain, stone, low cottages, sea,
a three foot smile, the brow of an empty road.

Phlegmatic

She rattles her choked ribs
up from graffitied streets,
where sentences that roam market walls
and hoardings round stored land
read like the stale breath of banked air,

to where spray won't be penned,
paint finds no purchase,
and claims spelt out in mass footfall
proved heartier than purse or word.

Here at the wet-lashed gape
of this caged lung she hears it:
bluster and fall, trickled whisper
to broad-throated roar;
feels its spit brush her,
stroke her clear.

Flight from Cuthbert Bank

from an autumn art walk
with Emilie Taylor and Mark Doyle

In search of pigeon lofts
we cross Philadelphia Park where gusted leaves
from laden crab apple trees chase over the scrub,
seed-blown flower heads ball into skeleton fists,
and my palms itch when dock-spikes rustle
their bright cluster-crust.

Some of us have memory-maps
to share, so we retrace how Wales Road's end
met the rise of Kelvin's *streets in the sky* –
a short-lived try to flat-stack a neighbourhood.

Then to the hillside opposite
we turn our gaze, led by the potter who sketched,
in slip and scraffito, men's pigeon-kept hearts
on the shoulders of vases a child could hide in;
wood-kiln fired them, carried both down from the sky
and its edge to plinth-rest in the hallowed half-dark
of the city's main art shed.

Under instruction, out on the path,
we ink-roll glass to catch the skyline: phone mast,
overgrown ski slope, Pitsmoor's Church of Christ
– all in reverse and smudge-edged; find a line
or word to mirror-write, hail each other's art,
then bag it up to head down Neepsend clough.

We skirt the six-lane race,
part thin trees to tread the dumped gear – teapot, tyre,
paint tin, plastic chair – that bolsters the soft rot
of fallen weed flesh, spent wood, topped
by a slither of leaves, waxen and wet.

When later we wheel
round and back up to peer over that top road wall,
we'll see how these flaking roof terraces nestle
in rhododendron and yellowing birch; lean further
for a bird's eye view of fly-bundled rubble sacks
where brazen new window frames lounge;
bramble and buddleia bind it all back.

Down at the foothills
we clutch creeper-twigs as we climb to the lofts.
Their ledges, when timing those loaded returns,
must have been like massive grins, each tooth a bird,
now collapsed to grimaces, above the faded bloom
of panels tagged in urban-runic fonts,

bedded in, weathered,
rooted like they grew there in the tangle-shrub.
A couple seem to topple from the bank, one has lost
its horizontal hold, is derailed so shifted slats
leer over the drop, its cabin-body lodged
in dented trees, shaggy in grassroots,
its gape creased shut.

Ten years since the last
kept pigeon homed to here. Back five more decades
to before they razed Parkwood Spring and sucked
Neepsend dry: the valley not this fleck of factory,
a filament between car galleries
and abandoned hillside,

but like a Lowry vision: a flock
of men released by work clocks, to rise above
day's end, the valley's din, legacies of grind,
to hold the small bulk, feel its heat
pulse through feathers in cupped hands,
and send those tiny hearts and lungs
to claim their reach of sky.

Star

They sit on the beach as day leaves the sky
his arm around her, telescope bright in his mind.
Before them the turn of the tide
behind them the old flint wall then the road.

In the dregs of the pier's sodium glow, locals fish
with a claw in a coin-slot cage
for watches and rings too sleek to grip.
While below in the geometry of girders
bladderwrack hangs like ribbons of held breath.

Sea shrugs and winks, sand shifts,
broken shells fall between stones.
From where the backwash laps at their feet
out to the seethe at her gaze's reach,
she measures the heave
listens for rhymes in its writhe and lash.

He's watching the sky

– *look* – pulls her round in time – *shooting star!*
Some stellar remnant trails its endgame blaze
through the double-you of Cassiopeia – a light-arc
in our atmosphere, seared now
over histories of suns lifetimes apart.

Gulls keen and dive, their wings
write the day's last light on sea's wrinkled skin.
Depth of field comes in waves light-years deep.
We are rain she says. *Stardust made flesh* says he.

They stay for one more cigarette
held by the shimmer of night's early risers
on swell that begins to suck back.

Slick pebbles gush.

Shedding sand, crosshatched by dusk
they lead longer shadows up from the shore.
The house with no dark corners grows small.
Inside she's sister and daughter,
a cake's lit with sixteen flames
and she blows.

Flickers

In a shaky hand you write
non-sequiturs then let the notebook fall.
Half your face has been folded away

a bruise blooms close to your brow
and white ruffles your throat's new inroad.
You are edited, pared down.

A pale coil leads your rhythm under
the lightness of you, from a clip on your toe,
to a staccato of spikes on a screen you can't see.

A younger you, new to me, sits by you, smiles
your smile, speaks your missing voice,
does what she can with the pillows.

My breath was clouds out in the early dusk,
ducks huddled fluffed up on grass-frost,
in here it's glasshouse-hot.

You seize the grape hyacinth I bring
and greedily palm its earth-cool pot, pick off
a leaf to push at your chapped lips.

But when your tacit glance flickers, I see you:
bone at the reach of a wound
melt-water clear in the spine of a frozen brook.

Losing Face

It's been ten minutes
since she trusted the spark-out

spark-it button. Now the oven
keeps its cool counsel.

There's a row of empty mouths
but she's running ahead –
half her head's at the hustings.

She reaches for matches

and in a breath
a flame-ball flash licks her,

stars flicker and fall from her hair,
skin-petals cling then unpeel

a blistering sheen
no one's meant to see.

Sea View

When her youngest takes everything
he can't pack to Oxfam and heads
at first light for Inverness, she weeps
into the wrinkled shine of late summer sand,
listens to shingle hiss the receding tide,
and buries her heart in a cheek-shaped hollow
cold in the Sussex flint.

*

When her kindest lover yet hears enough
he shoves his full plate like a snooker shot:
Christmas crockery smashed in her lap,
and the rest of what may've sustained them
splatters her flat.

Caught on the icy back stair,
tight-lipped in slippers, she bites her tongue
clean off, sees it sizzle down to the shore
where it steams itself in the shallows.

*

When her last friends drift, they wave.
She turns away, slips into scuffed kitten heels
to sling back gins at a windswept bar

till all she's left is a rust-licked wall to climb.
Sea swallows stars and iron steps bleed,
serve her again up to another night's blur.
She stands by the breadth of her bed
stares out the thickening pane, on the swell,
dark, still fresh.

Last night

                    mist rolled in –
a settlement of pale net layered itself
on the hillside opposite, and sagged
into gardens and lanes, bleared terraces
of gable-ends, nestling in to stifle all
but its own rumour, letting only the pin-glow
of street and window lights poke through.
It flattened valleys, lagged farm and woodland,
swallowed Dark Peak and Bradfield's mound
into a sky white with it, tasted our tongues
as we talked of it, beaded our hair and lashes.

Morning sloshes in gutters,
pelts tarmac with its urgent gurgle-hiss,
the radio gushes flood warnings.
I peer out through the weft and warp
of our rain-braided window on mud
leaping puddles in grass and gravel,
Walkley Stream overflowing its runnel,
potholes filling to discharge in gulleys
down our road's ribbed gradient,
and last night's mist, slow to thin
in its outpouring, still fleeces us
of field's depth: near hills show as bones,
roof and tree lines seem sketched
in charcoal on translucent stone.

Loop

Physic

I draw your shudder close, force a breach
in zipped-up fur, probe black lip-flesh
for a finger's width to prise apart your jaw,
feel your mouth's roof-ridges
like boat timbers or a whale's ribcage.
You gnash and tremble, loose inside your fur
yet secure as I dodge molars, grapple
with your saliva-slick muscle,
to rest the tablet in your gag reflex
then slip out and grab your greying muzzle,
hold it closed, howl-raised, stroke your throat
until you swallow. I pull you near
while the tremor slips away,
you stare ahead, shoulder in my breast.

Road

These are dark dog days.
You wear the film-star coat

fur on fur, rib around your shaven ribs.
We drive the old steel road alone

flanked by the corrugated rust
of screened vacated plots.

Lode

Here is the field
walled from the road

here is the shovel and here's the hole
we dug in the slant of the sun

Here is the new-turned soil
here is the pile of exigent stones

pulled from the earth
here is the two-square of turf

Here are the berries from home
here the bundle of bone and fur

Hear the weep of the burn
bleeding the peat-brown last week's rain

over the limestone laying it down
leaching it into the loam

Here is the blanket light of her
now is the season's turn

here are the long-night logs and leaves
here's where the basket burns

Impasse

The bone in her heart grows up past her throat
crackles its chill in her

                stone cold cheek

she can't talk it away so she walks it
down by the river's raw bite.

She stalks the rimy bank of a tongue
for where water will wear away bone
each footstep following one of her own.

On shale, under blear, limestone chains
lie like spines in the shallow gravel bed.

Snagged in rock at a weir's head, a dog-leg
of thorn-rusted twig, hoar-coated

in feathers like bleached iron filings, clings
to robin-red hips hard-glazed

                in the current's breath.

Now the blood's in her belly

the sleet in her chest hacks up, grist
to her grind, spits out over her lip's crust.

Spume crests the bitter flow

                melt swells.

By the lee path she leaves riven depths, treks
through woods' winter skeletons, broaches the burn

to the ice field, stone still.

Allotment

While you rake our fire's remains, you tell me
of glazed, ruffled clowns these terraces keep
on yielding: scathed and startled, unearthed in beds
like raised dead, ashen to their grit-stained faces.

Last night we burned dug-up tree stumps,
rotten wood, choked bramble, dirt-clogged rags,
leaves, brittle mats of lifeless hair-sprung root.
Then you shoved on the weather-blown shed
and its parting breaths seemed to lick the stars.

Now, as you hold up the china figure found
spread-eagled to the sky on the charred pile,
clouds bank and fill: the storm begins its slow pull in.

And when you scoop a sieveful to sift for metal,
clinker, bits of clown, you riddle anti-clockwise,
send a fine tornado coiling the earth back home.

Path Kill

After several days,
between outcrops of fur
and its silvery moss remains,
a pouch, bin-bag black,
creases at the underbelly
like a baby's wrist,
still foetal, kidney-shaped,
held from dew and rain.

Woodlouse and fly families later,
flat-stacked in fraying layers
dog-eared rug-matted black
leaf-like in leaves, secret
in bramble and buttercup,
ransacked, leaching back.

Tumour

Behind the consultant, a lone slub of cloud
bruised mountain grey, the weight of continents
framed in the aging sky.

Pinned to the wall: a map,
two labelled hemispheres flapping
in the evening's drift.

He swims the light he brings

held in air between his skin and skin,
in hair his own lit corridor, he's braced
to face the heft of this domain,
knows his place in the hierarchy of gravity
is with the surface tension, yet he ripples,
hears chattering like rain in waves

as cells of luminance unravelled
and sprung breath rise to slip away;
in fists his finger tissues meet,
as feet fuse into flippers
he realises a river's in his veins,

remembers stories of gnomes re-homed
below the scree of Scafell Pike
down beyond the law's long arm,
who vent their lure as rumour
sent up to ferment in divers' minds,

and the ocean floor off Grenada,
once layered-lush, now fleeced,
where children, cast in fibreglass and vested
in cement, are holding hands, each calcifies,
each preserves the porous, the adaptive,
inhabiting the barren brine as colonnades
to sustain every raid by a new coral reef.

In search of neurons, prenatal or fallow
since we left the sea,
he plunders his brain's ravines
for gills and tentacles, for scales
instead of skin, he dreams a fin.

Not thistledown

Don't clothe me in polished death
and sing me to the flame
or spill me on a favourite field
pieces squandered to the rinse of rain.

Bag me up in hand-me-downs
lay my last bed in the ground
rest my bone-work in oak root's way.
Sing then, if it would make the day.

Notes and Acknowledgements

When we're fluent... was commissioned by Ruth Nutter for the 2015 *Ruskin in Sheffield* programme.

Goat Boy and Other Journeys The character in Susannah Gent's installation *Piss Take*, at Bank Street Arts, Sheffield, gave me Goat Boy's voice, then discussion with Gent enabled 'Taxidermy for Beginners' and 'How We Came to This'. Further collaboration produced a film and poetry performance piece for Sheffield Poetry Festival 2013. Our subsequent collaboration with Linda Lee Welch and The Only Michael spurred 'Goat Boy staggers on', and a multimedia performance piece for Off the Shelf 2013.

Pulling Balsam tells of fending off the invasive species Himalayan balsam. Further background to this and other poems can be found in 'Contra Flow', an essay for the Longbarrow Blog (posted 9 April 2014).

Memoir of a Working River is set on the River Rivelin, with historical and industrial information gleaned from: *Water Power on the Sheffield Rivers* by Ball, Crossley and Flavell; *Walking the Rivelin* by Sue Shaw and Keith Kendall; *The Condition of the Working Class 1844* by Friedrich Engels.

Flood Triptych: The Loxley At midnight, 11th March 1864, the newly constructed Dale Dyke Dam burst, sending 700 million gallons of water down the Loxley at around 30mph, killing over 250 people, wrecking all homes and works for eight miles. These poems emerged from walks along the flood's course, taken with photographer Joshua Holt. Further river walks taken with photographer Karl Hurst, on which we discussed work and nature, land and class, led to Hurst making images from the poetry sequence, and producing the boxed edition also titled 'Flood Triptych: The Loxley'. The story told in 'Little Matlock' takes elements from several episodes in Samuel Harrison's *A Complete History of the Great Flood at Sheffield*, published in 1864.

Phlegmatic is an ekphrastic response to Paul Evans's painting *Kinder Downfall*, commissioned by Longbarrow Press for *The Seven Wonders* project.

Flight from Cuthbert Bank tells of an autumn art walk through the Sheffield districts of Upperthorpe and Walkley, led by Mark Doyle and Emilie Taylor, with images and influence from Taylor's ceramic vases, exhibited at Sheffield's Millennium Gallery as *So High I Almost Touch The Sky*.

He swims the light he brings is an ekphrastic response to a photograph by Tom Hyde, commissioned by Angelina D'Roza for her Catalyst project at Bank Street Arts. The poem refers to garden gnomes apparently placed in the depths of Scafell Pike, and to 'Viccisitudes', an ocean bed sculpture by Jason deCaires Taylor.

*

For their help in writing these poems, I'm grateful to: Matthew Clegg, Angelina D'Roza, Andy Hirst, Matt Black, Rob Hindle, Chris Jones, Cat Lowell, Maurice Riordan, and all members, past and present, of Tuesday Poets. I'm indebted to Brian Lewis for his rigour, flair, and true collaborative spirit.

Very special thanks as ever to Graeme Hodgson, Mary Musselwhite, Claire Fuller.

In memory of my parents Jan and Roy Musselwhite.